DEAR VALUED CUST

Thank you for choosing to shop with us! We are grateful for your trust and support. Your satisfaction is our top priority and we hope you had a positive experience with us.

If you're happy with your purchase, please consider leaving us a review on Amazon. Your feedback helps us continue to provide the best products and service to our valued customers like you.

BRIGHTEN YOUR DAY WITH COLOR!

Life can be tough, and taking care of our mental well-being is more important than ever. The stress of recent years has hit us all hard, which is why diving into art has become a key way to relax and find a little joy.

PAPER SELECTION

We go with standard-quality paper because it's easier on the wallet, especially with limited options on Amazon. To avoid any ink bleed-through from your pens or markers, just slide a thicker blank sheet behind the page you're coloring. Thanks for rolling with us on this choice!

SHOW OFF YOUR ART

Since our Adult Coloring Books hit Amazon, we've seen so many of you bring these pages to life with your amazing creativity. When you leave a review, feel free to share some pictures of your work—we'd love to celebrate your art with you! Can't wait to see what you've created! 😊

CONNECT WITH US

For any concerns, please feel free to contact us at **support@hotholic.com**

Follow us: **@hotholic**

LADA NIVA

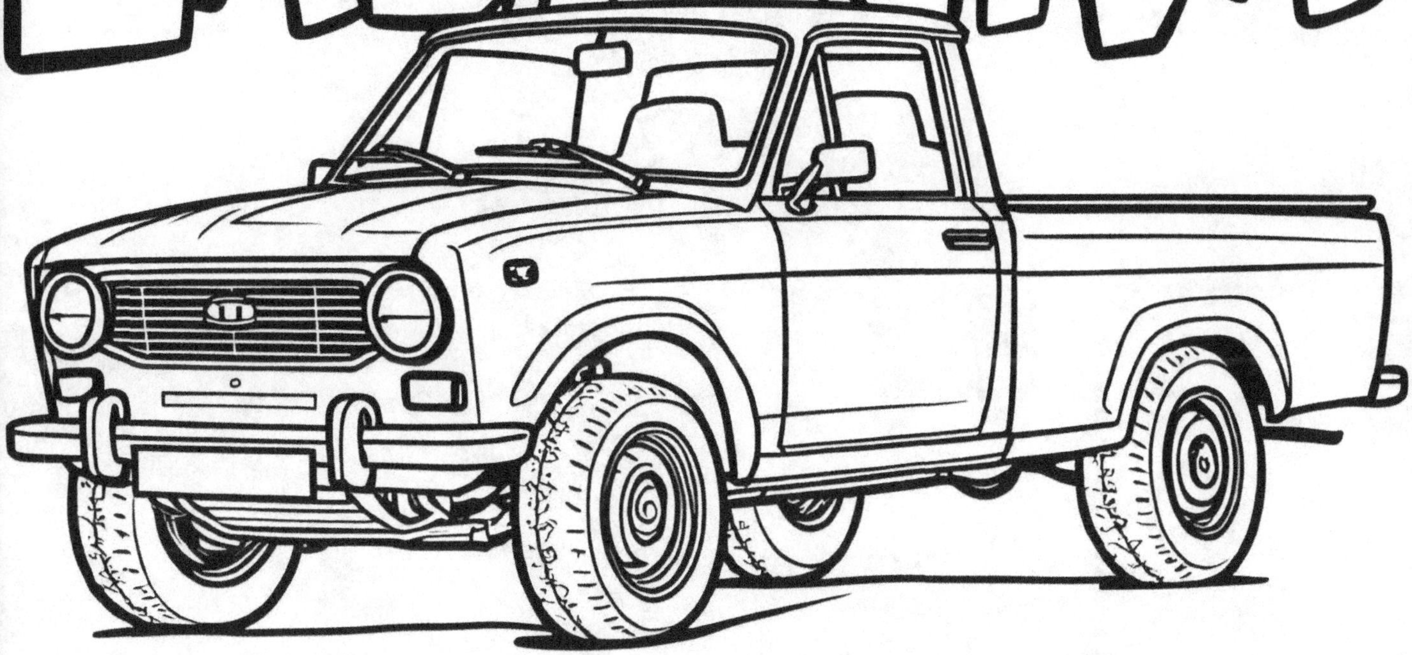

Runabout

Daily 4x4

HILUX

Sport Trac

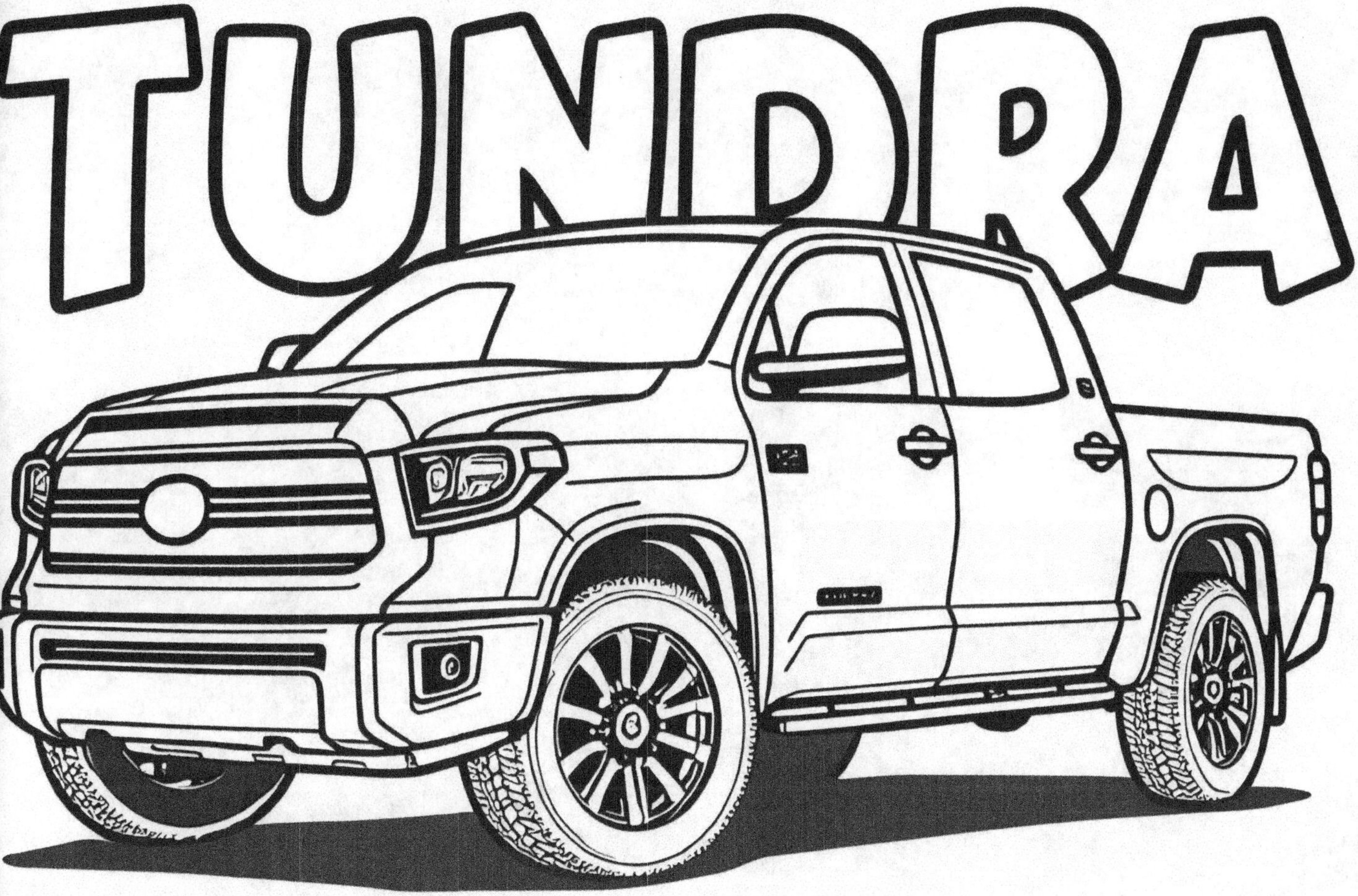
TUNDRA

SYCLONE

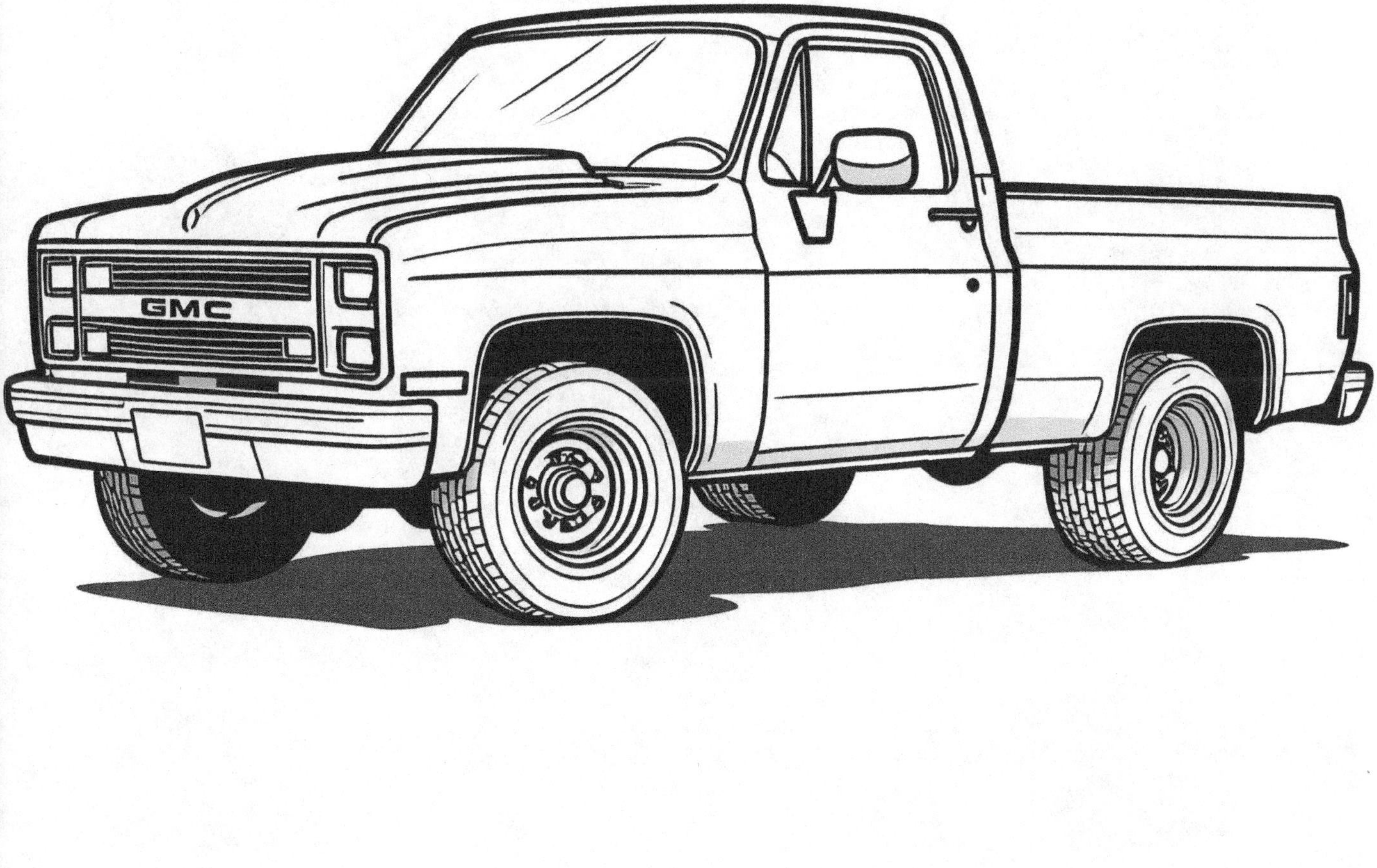

Sweptside

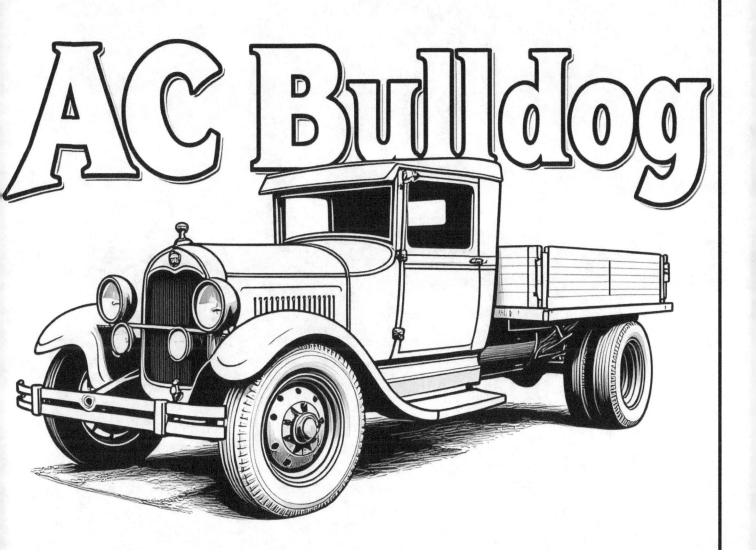

Made in the USA
Las Vegas, NV
19 November 2024

12146988R00057